- *DAD THE REAL HERO / BY NIKHIL MHATRE*

Name: NIKHIL VISHNU MHATRE

words count:

-

EMAIL ID: nickmhatre@1295gmail.com

CONTACT NO: 8976161895

DAD THE REAL HERO

(BY NIKHIL MHATRE)

1. WHO IS DAD

DAD is the only person in the world, who love you more than Himself. HE is the only person, who think about

Our future every moments.

HE is best friend for life. He will always be with you, no matter in which problem's we are. That's why no one can take his place in our life

Even in times of failure, His the only one who tells Us

- ***DAD THE REAL HERO / BY NIKHIL MHATRE***

"You can do it."

HE holds special value in our life. HE is the One of best guiding hand ever, & He will give our life right way.

He is very special man. If you have dad you are so lucky, because some people doesn't have their parents. Thus know the more value of having parents better than others.

Dad is like diamond but this diamond is in raw form and you have to find out. That diamond hidden behind the Strictness and hardness which he always show's us. So that we should stay on the path of his footprints. To live social and secureness with moral values of life.

"You may ignore him today but you can't afford to lose him tomorrow"

He is precious, nobody can name value of father.

There are not enough words to explain about him...

DAD will give best experience of success and faith to face failure's to us and its helps us to survive in our life. He never run's away from his responsibility. He always come forward to take a charge of his responsibility.

He is symbol of being accountable liabilities. He does everything in a good way and that makes him very special man.

Dad the person in your life who wants to give you all those things. That he never had in his life. The only person who sees your problems as his Own, but Others can only show you condolence, but there only person who puts his entire effort to solve your problem that's dad for you

Being a dad isn't about to have family. It is about to have responsibilities. Not only at home, but in world. Dad the only who punishes you scolds you. Not because he wants to hurt you. But he does to make you good Learner. There are millions of people will love you but the way he loves you nobody can.

Dad his role in your is very vital, maybe today you don't have any idea about his role. But you will realise when you stand in his place at a certain stage of life, you surely realise, he is a hero of your life

DAD is the great mentor for you. Because only he knows you very well. He knows your each and every habits and he can handle you easily and understand you & your feelings too. But he also need your attention I believe that getting mentorship from him is like getting mentorship from god.

He possess some fantastic quality in himself and those quality you need to build in yourself. There is no doubt about it. He keeps himself very well & also teach you how to present yourself to others. Dad always assist you in everything with knowing that you need his help.

Dad every time wants to see you happy, the one who looks at your happiness as his & your problem as his and he never complains about anything. He works harder & harder but never give up. He fall's and stands.

This happened again & again but he never give up.

This is best quality of his. The kind of fighting spirits he has nobody does such thing that. Understand him.

"DAD IS THE ONLY PERSON IN YOUR LIFE, WHO WORK FOR YOU"

There are many examples of his importance and you would see that easily. Many people are dying for dad.

- ***DAD THE REAL HERO / BY NIKHIL MHATRE***

Dad is amazing person and it is almost impossible to anyone to explain the word dad. Dad isn't person, his a gift, a blessing, a shadow of god. He corrects your all mistakes.

Dad is fills up emptiness in your life. Dad try his best to complete your every wish, dad only could be like that in your life.

'He is a creator of your life'

Dad is the only person who comes forward to solve your problem. He is playing various role your life, according to needs of your life.

- ***DAD THE REAL HERO / BY NIKHIL MHATRE***

Being a dad he plays many role in your life but, you will always be unaware about that. You may think He does nothing for you. He is kind of personality even he who every time take difficult role in act of life. As a back bone of your life, he is life line of your life.

'DAD ISNT JUST PERSON, IT'S A HUGE PERSONALITY'

Not everyone is lucky in this world. There are so many people who is praying for him. But he shows unconditional love every moments of his life maybe be sometime he shouted at you loudly but there is worry behind his shout. You couldn't understand even he put many restrictions on you, but the intention was very clear your safety and then you get nervous, at that moment he come and try to appreciate your feelings. It's a very beautiful to see him to appreciating your feelings and he does it very well.

And our fight end up with smile. The dad does everything for you but couldn't see unhappy you.

He could be in problem but never let you in problem, he would be unhappy but never would see you unhappy that's a dad for you .....

- ***DAD THE REAL HERO / BY NIKHIL MHATRE***

Believe that you couldn't be what you are today without him. Your life is like blank canvas and dad is like colours

He fill colours in your life, he give meaning to your life.

He always be behind you, that's true just see your name you get your answer. Dad is like someone whom you hate as much as you love. Dad just want see you more successful than him then he attempt different, different way to drop you there

- ***DAD THE REAL HERO / BY NIKHIL MHATRE***

Many of you confuse to understand him, weather he is guiding or commanding you, but this is not true dad always guiding you and never dream about commanding you

He is such great personality, you may not accept that right now.

Today your living such a beautiful life just Because of him he never show his pain. Such a strong man he is.

He face challenges every moments but never

complaint that or say that he is in trouble. Whenever you ask him how is life going he say everything fine.

This is the most difficult task he done for you and it is never easy to be positive at the when he is in negative moments but he done it very well... that's dad for you

Dad isn't about to have teacher, he is great mentor.

He always teach you such a good skills like

- *The Art of dealing with people*
- *Communication*

- ***DAD THE REAL HERO / BY NIKHIL MHATRE***
- *Keep yourself fully fit & active*
- *Project yourself as a personality*
- *Give cute smile while saying hello*

These skills are very common but very effective

To putting positive impact on others.

In form of Dad you get true friend for life. The Best answering machine for your every questions.

Dad is like google you get every information from him about your life. This is the best way tell his value to today's generation that

2. LOVE

Dads love is like air you couldn't see but you could feel it. His love is always keep this thing secrets, he never able show you how much he loves you. That's why you think that he isn't love you.

The only person in your life who love more than himself. You call him dad nobody could have such amounts of love for you that he has for you.

Many people love you for a while but only he would love forever and it's appear every time in his action how much he love you but you have to appreciate your dad.

Then your relationship bond get stronger with unbreakable shelf.

Your bond keep your relationship stronger than before. Dads love is a like anti dote for you. You get good result when you need that anti dote.

Exactly same happened with dad unless you need his love, this would never work for you.

You never know how emotional he is, He every time wants to tell how much love but couldn't tell because he doesn't want to be emotional in front of you.

Dad is not only name its symbol of being accountable

He love you forever nobody would love you the way

he love you, getting his love is like getting love from god.

You may not accept it now but one day you must accept it. His love is very precious. Very few people get it.

Dad loves is unexplainable, we couldn't explain in the words about his love, his love is 100% true and you get true love only from him. He spend entire life to fulfil your dream.

- *The best gift for every daughter*

Dads love is best gift for every daughter. The bonding between dad & daughter is unbreakable. That's why.

- *DAD THE REAL HERO / BY NIKHIL MHATRE*

"*Dads love is the oxygen for every girl* "

What is love you should ask any girl, she would tell you much better

Dads smile is much sweeter than sugar for every girl. His love gets more value for girls when daughter and dad come together then the whole world shine that's the power of these two have.

For the every girl dads love is needs of their life. Girls couldn't be without dads love, this is special quality of dads love.

Dads love matter much than others for every girls

- ***DAD THE REAL HERO / BY NIKHIL MHATRE***

There is only one person's love they need most that's dad's love.

Dad the only person who is loving you selflessly. His love is more expensive than diamond.

The diamond maybe catch your attraction, but his love May understand your emotions. Many people talk about him but very few people match his level. Dad's love is far beyond your imagination.

Dad is like computer and his love like software but your relationship with him, Is the key to start this programme. If there is enough amounts of love then this programme keep on forever.

There isn't any measurement tools that count amounts of love and this is impossible to create such tool like that count amounts of love.

The entire world need his love there is nothing like his love.

I believe that his love has magical effects on you. In terms of being true loving person for you. There is only dad for you.

Dads love first then others for every girl. No matter how busy todays girls in their studies, work or something but they always need his love, they missing him a lot.

The dad is the first hero for every girl then they see him as a dad. But every girl see him as hero.

We don't have idea about, how much important

his love for every girl. Dads love is everything for every girl.

We never calculate how much important girl has for his love.

But dad is first male person in the universe with every girl comfortable. There is something special in his that's why.

Dads love is one of the most expensive thing in the world but you couldn't buy it just like you buy other things, his love is also your life achievement because today also many people still searching his love.

This is what his love hold value in your life. You couldn't imagine about his love.

Dads love is a like sun, you maybe hate sun in summer but you may like sun in winter. You change your thoughts according to the condition of your life.

Exactly same thing happened with him too. You realize value of his love according to the time and understand it too.

The parson who is loving you more than himself, he deserve to be special in your life. Unless you are getting his love you don't need to be worry because dad's love has power to protect you every time.

- ***DAD THE REAL HERO / BY NIKHIL MHATRE***

Dad's love is not available in world's any market. His love is very rare to get and we are using this line many times every day I can buy everything but there some things today also we can't buy,

We can only earn them. Earning dad's love is biggest achievement of my life.

Because I realize my life would be nothing without him.

He distribute amounts of love in our family. He is such talented person. Great human being.

You and I can never be like him. Dad would be dad Nobody would be like him.

- ***DAD THE REAL HERO / BY NIKHIL MHATRE***

The only parson who is fulfilling your life through huge amounts of love that's dad for you.

Only he could does such things for you, others would promise or commitment but he is the only one who is make it true. Be a grateful for his love

"DAD IS THE SOURSE OF LOVE"

3. DEDCATION

Dad is the best person to teach everyone the value of dedication. Being dedicated means what he would show you, how dedicated he is towards his work and responsibility.

He is the only one guy who is dedicated himself for you without expecting any returns from you.

Dad's contribution in your life is huge. You never imagine about his contribution at all and it's true

"THERE ARE SOME PERSONALITY NEVER EXIST AGAIN AND YOUR DAD IS ONE OF THEM "

- ***DAD THE REAL HERO / BY NIKHIL MHATRE***

This is the Reason why I am telling you guys, your dad never going to back again so be grateful for his dedication in your life.

Your dad is like diamond and many industries using diamond cutters for hard material cutting exactly same act your dad does in your life.

He cut your all difficulties and give you sharp shape Dad this ward itself say dedicated action to dream.

He always be dedicated to your dream even you lose your hope but he keep trying to chasing your dream. And make it happened for you.

- ***DAD THE REAL HERO / BY NIKHIL MHATRE***

He dedicated himself fully, he spent his entire life towards his responsibility and successfully complete them, he is star icon for the world and he always take smart action on everything that's make him star icon in the world, dad is the real star icon of your life.

He deserve to be star icon in your life. Because of his work, dedication give him that special degree this degree is much more valuable than other degrees'

Because this degree is all about dedication towards your responsibility and very few people get it but your dad is one of them and many people couldn't be dedicated towards themselves.

Dad also teaching you dedication and how important to be dedicate towards your gaols or something you wanted to achieve.

"BEING DEDICATED TOWARDS YOUR RESPONSIBILITY IS THE EQUAL BEING HONEST TO YOURSELF "

Dad's dedication is true and honest there no doubt about his dedication.

"Dedication is the first step towards becoming the good human being" and this is very important to everyone how dedicate your

When question is about who is dedicate themselves to improving your life. The answer is only your dad.

How dedicate he is to his responsibility.

This is enough to know about his passionate towards his dedication.

He is first person who does that remember your dad is your helping hand and he dedicate himself to improve your life.

"Dad this ward itself say dedication and determination"

Being dedicate & determine Dad is all about. He keep focus on his work and never distract by any obstruction.

The way he dedicate himself towards his work and

responsibility is remarkable but he never stop here.

He always ready to accept new challenge and he keeping smart attitude in his mind that's make him special person.

He always respond to the challenges positively and his positive attitude every time give him valuable lessons.

He is the best, not just because he handle challenges very well but even he gets more strength from the challenges.

This is the best thing about his dedication. He isn't only dedicating himself. He getting many valuable things through his dedication.

That's why he is the best. He teaching you how to utilize your time. He does multitasking very well.

Every day he work more than his ability. Every time he is putting extra efforts in daily work, he dose over time, he sacrifice his small, small Wish's for you. He does everything for you. Even still you think he doesn't care for you. You have no idea.

"Your today's happiness behind reason your dad's yesterday's huge dedication"

The only reason why you are getting happiness in your life.

There is one gentleman and his Dedication serving you happiness that's dad for you.

- *DAD THE REAL HERO / BY NIKHIL MHATRE*

Could you imagine how many people would dedicate themselves for you and the way your dad does for you.

If you see there is nobody would come forward to be dedicate for you.

Dad's dedication speak everything about his love, care, value he has for you in his life.

Many people say you are my friend, best friend, brother, sister or whatever they say but its verbal relation but never forget with your dad its blood relation.

Many relation you made and break in your life but the only relation would stay with you forever and this is unbreakable relationship between you and your dad.

This how he also dedicate himself in relationship. He take dedication on different level. He show how important dedication in relationship too.

“***You are life line for your dad***”

Dedication is all about being focus on your work, responsibility, and making sure your good being human.

He dedicate himself rest of his life. Being truly dedicate to his responsibility and showing to the whole how cool he is, he prove himself as the being dedicate isn’t joke its sing of being mature.

Maturity is about to be capable to take responsibility, capable to manage everything by themselves and ready to solve the problems this what dad dedicate himself.

He always ready to solve problems of your and others too.

He always be cool no matter which condition he is facing this what he is having positive attitude that's only matter in life.

Because his attitude helping him in dedication and his attitude drive him crazy to dedicate himself the way nobody could.

Dad is the only person in your life who is dedicating every moments of his life to improve your life. His dedication always going to you. He never dedicate for him.

He always dedicate for you. There is nobody could match his dedication level. His level beyond your imagination.

I always pray to god keep safe to the all dad's.
I feel dad is smart person he always come forward to accept responsibility and even he is having huge responsibility on his head he behave like nothing is on his head.

He knows his role very well and he will play too

I never forget your dedication dad. This best gift you have given me. Because whatever today am I just because dad your huge dedication.

I never tell you what you have done for me but really you're the best.

4. SACRIFICE

Sacrifice is the first priority of dad's life. Being dad is huge task for him. There are many role he has to play in your life.

As a dad he has to fulfil your every wish's, every desire and your wish's desire complete through sacrifice.

He has to go through the sacrifice to fulfil your every desire. Dad is the only person in your life who sacrifice for you every time. He never mind but does that happily because he know that his sacrifice get reworded by your happiness. He sacrifice only for your happiness.

- ***DAD THE REAL HERO / BY NIKHIL MHATRE***

Dad the person whom your happiness is the first duty.

The first activity he want to dose in the every morning serving happiness to you through the action. This is the very first activity he want to dose in the every morning and it is never easy to him also but he forget everything and begin his day serving happiness to you. This seem like small thing but its means a lot more than anything.

There is nobody would think about begin your day through the happiness but there is always one person who dose that's dad for you.

This kind of small, small sacrifice he make every day for you. You are totally unaware about that his sacrifice giving your life shine. He burning himself and giving shine to you. The only person in your life who has guts to do this for you.

Dad who is carry you in his mind forever and fulfil happiness your life through his sacrifice, dedication, and love.

"BEING DAD IS THE MASSTER DEGREE OF YOUR LIFE" & "SACRIFICE IS THE KEY TO GET THIS DEGREE"

This degree is much more precious than gold because you need true feelings. You couldn't purchase this degree. You have to earn by your sacrifice like your dad dose. Sacrifice is one of the huge reason today also humanity is alive and its start from you. How many times sacrifice for you and for your better future. Or others.

"Sacrifice is the best way to show someone, how much you love them"

Everyday your dad showing you how much he love you. When he sacrifice for you and his intention to see you being successful. This is the reword for him, for his huge sacrifice. Your action must be enough to show him how much you love him too.

Dad is the only person in your life who is give up many things for you. Our life without him and his sacrifice is like blank canvas and we know that there is no value for blank canvas, when canvas get colours on it then canvas gets meaning for its colours exactly same meaning we get From his sacrifice.

Dad's sacrifice giving true colours to your life. He always make sure that you would be happy forever that's what dad dose for you.

There are many people dying for him. Many people praying for him. Because he is very strong man and he is very kind hart, sensitive, emotional and most important HE IS A GENTLEMAN...

Sacrificing for someone that's show how much value & importance you have for them and dad sacrificing from before your birth. Dad sacrifice his every desire to complete your every desire.

He has the massive will power and he make many sacrifice easily because of his will power, his will make him strong person and not only his will make him strong but he possess many beautiful qualities that's make him strong and special.

He has many qualities but there is qualities make him very special is that "sacrifice" this is one of the great reason. He hold special place in your life.

He play various role in your life according to needs of your life. There is nothing beautiful than his sacrifice because he make it from hart of his bottom. True feeling, quality love and many more superior things he give you

Today you seeing love, happiness, enjoy just because of his sacrifice. Sacrifice is of the best gift that your dad giving you from many years.

He is the only one who could dose that others would say but he is the only who make it true. There is massive different between dad & others. Dad is diamond & others are gold.

You could rebuild gold but you never rebuild diamond

because once diamond breaks then diamond would burst. There isn't any other option to rebuild it.

Only one option you have to keep it safe & protect forever there is only one choice either you keep safe it & protect forever or lose it.

He always think about you. He giving up many times in single day. He give up his small & big desire too but he is not only giving up for you many times in single day but he try his best to fulfil your wish.

- ***DAD THE REAL HERO / BY NIKHIL MHATRE***

Dad who brings chocolate to happiness each and everything he mange somehow but don't say no to you he borrow money from others to purchase those things that he promise to you. He would give to you. Its look like small thing but it has much value for him.

Fulfilling your desire is the first duty of his life and you call him dad.

Behind every good moments of your life there is His huge sacrifice.

There are many people give up for you, but there is

only one person who truly sacrifice for you that's dad.

There is huge difference between dad's sacrifice & other people give up for you. Other people would give up things they like for you, few times but would show or remind you many times, dad would sacrifice every time for you but never remind or show that's dad for you.

The difference between dad & others is very clear. Your dad sacrifice for you and work for your goals.

- ***DAD THE REAL HERO / BY NIKHIL MHATRE***

There is nobody like him. He is special guy and he looking at your gaols as his gaols, he help you achieving your gaols.

Dad always be with you no matter how terrible situation in you are but he never leave you alone this is the reason he is best because best person never let anyone alone in terrible situation that's sing of being best and great.

But it is not easy like you say, for this you have to be dedicate, sacrifice, will power to be best. And dad dose it very well

He sacrifice happily for you and never does anything for credit. He does everything as responsibility & duty.

There is one best person who sacrifice for you but never say anything because his sacrifice is true, he sacrifice to take you forward not backward, and only he could think like that. That's what dad for you.

Dad's huge contribution in your life. He contribute in everything weather it would be your basic needs educational, social, or personal his huge contribution in these needs of your life.

He always contributing for you in various way sometime he does over time to get extra money to bring the things you wanted. He avoid purchasing things he wants for you.

He hide his pain behind his smile for you. He wake up early in the morning and rush on duty without taking tiffin, he forget many things in the morning just he has to reach at office on the time. He fighting with time every moments of his life.

- ***DAD THE REAL HERO / BY NIKHIL MHATRE***

He does fight with time. His life is like clock every time he is moving, thinking but he keep himself very well. It doesn't matter he is in problem or not. But you every time see smile on his face that's what how strong he is mentally too

"Being dad is all about being gentleman"

He is great human being, great guiding hand and one of the best person in the world.

He does many things in his whole life. He dedicate his whole life for you.

- ***DAD THE REAL HERO / BY NIKHIL MHATRE***

He never stop his work even you get young keep working to fulfil your small desire. Every time he think about your future and put his whole effort to give you better lifestyle.

The way he does everything is remarkable and you must appreciate him. He always show his class in his action. He very classy guy. Sometimes shouted at you, punish you but most important thing is he loves you. That's why he does that and you no idea how much hurt him when he see you sad or you get hurt because you are as important as like breath for him.

He couldn't show you or tell you about that but believe me. He is loving you more than himself.

He every time make compromise to complete your needs and you forget these small, small compromise he make every day for you and his small, small compromise give you huge happiness and this is very important to everyone know how many compromise your dad make in a single day to make your each day happy, it is not easy but he make it easy through his smart work.

Is there anyone is working for your happiness the one & only your dad so make sure he also be happy.

- ***DAD THE REAL HERO / BY NIKHIL MHATRE***

Don't only say dad are you happy work for his happiness and his one desire inspire him to work hard, sacrifice. That is see you successful in your life before he die. This is the only one desire he has but it is very sad and today's fact that many dad's desire stay only desire forever they leave this world with incomplete desire.

There are many dad who is sacrifice a lot his child doesn't have value for his sacrifice. The way treat dad its kill him alive and this is very painful than any other pain. His sacrifice coming from his heart of bottom, it is true sing of true relationship between you and your dad.

- ***DAD THE REAL HERO / BY NIKHIL MHATRE***

Dad always come forward to make compromise. He never take much time to make decision. He make it and work on to prove it right. Dad not only sacrifice for you.

He give your life right angle, right way to go forward and beyond that. His sacrifice is one of the best gift that you get because sacrifice is not thing that you could purchase for yourself. This is one of best gift you could give to someone and every dad giving this such best & great gift to their child and your dad also one of them.

- ***DAD THE REAL HERO / BY NIKHIL MHATRE***

Your happiness is the very first priority for him and he is the only person in your life who does that.

Let me tell you one story about dads sacrifice

There was one dad who is dedicating his each & every moments to make his son life better. He was very hard working man and very passionately doing his work.

He was putting his whole effort to brought happiness to his son life but his son doesn't have value for his sacrifice, dedication and love.

He was giving everything to his son but he wasn't

aware about his mistake because he was fulfilling his son needs but his son thought his dad getting everything easily.

After that his son expectation raise, his son demanding many expensive things even now also his dad manage somehow and complete.

But one day his dad don't complete his sons wish that day his shout at him and used very bad words, stared blaming him that his dad realize. He was too much protective. He didn't show his son how much effort he was putting for him.

5. EMOTION'S

Dad this person is symbol of being emotional and he is very different guy, he never show his emotion but this doesn't mean he isn't emotional. He is kind of guy who is not ready to accept that he is emotional whenever you ask him. He say he isn't emotional but why he is say that

The reason is clear to make sure that there is someone who is strong enough to solve your problems and motivate you to do what you want to do. He always hide his emotion from you as well from others too

- ***DAD THE REAL HERO / BY NIKHIL MHATRE***

He every time go forward to face problems and successfully solve every problems. And set lessons for every one

Dad if you want to see how dad could be emotional then you must see his eyes and maintain eye contact with him then you realises how emotional is he. When you get ill and you get hospitalise outside of room there is one gentleman who is praying for your life that's show how emotional he is maybe you haven't see such

Condition yet but you could see in any hospital there many dads who is praying for their kid life.

Dad the way he express his emotion to god its very

beautiful moments to see how emotion he is. But he has many responsibility. He has to be strong there is no choice front of at that moments and he does that well. He play his role very well even that moment. He handle situation well at that moments and himself too. He never crumble. He get strong whenever problems come. The way He maintain positive attitude that's unbelievable, there is nobody would keep themselves the dad keep himself in difficult situation.

How he control his emotion in every situation that's remarkable. He does many things and hide too. But emotion is such thing that's automatically come out

"DAD IS THE POWE HOUSE OF EMOTION"

You could express your emotion directly with anyone but what about dad. He is in kind of role in the film of life. Where he has to play many role's at same time. He play his role well and control whole situation and maintain right balance in family that's how he control his emotion and himself too.

He want to see everyone happy but when family in problem at that moment he get charge and rush to solve the problem. He keep everyone away from the problems and he face alone everything. Dad the only one person who sacrifice, dedicate, and love you from the day you born to till his last breath. He is the reason why you are getting respect from society and everyone.

He always want to see you doing well but when you are not doing its mean for him he isn't doing well, when you are fail for him like he fail. He is very excited about your success and his emotion joint with your progress but his emotion is extremely powerful that's drive him crazy to does something extraordinary for you and he make it happened that's dad for you

When he get emotional then his best performance

come out and he show to the whole world how emotional he is, how strong he is. He doesn't like to be emotional but some situations are very different and where everyone get emotional and he also get emotional too.

He realize that his family and you depends on him. If he stay emotional then it's become more difficult to handle the situation and he back again in normal form and successfully bring smile on everyone face even in such condition he mange it that's remarkable thing about him

He always does everything persistently then weather

work, love or his responsibility he does it well. When you shouted at him he gets emotional he doesn’t cry but his heart get burst in many parts and it’s very painful.

This pain has no painkiller exist yet that give him relief from pain.

The way he live his life it’s very difficult to anyone live life like him. There are many compromise he make in his entire life and it’s wasn’t easy but he make it for you. His emotions inspire him to make compromise and he doesn’t regret that. But he also need your love too

He doesn’t need money to be happy but he need your attention, those caring words and love from you and he deserve that your very first priority must be his happiness and his care then you see how he react on your behaver.

He would cry uncountable he show you how soft hearted he is.

How much emotion he was keep in his mind it’s all

expose that day when you show some respect to him and enough amounts of love to him

Dad the way he sacrifice, love, dedicate, and being emotional for you nobody could.

He is very loving and emotional person but there are many responsibility's on his head that's why he isn't showing his soft side. He has many desire but as dad he give up his all desire for you and try to fulfil your desire.

- ***DAD THE REAL HERO / BY NIKHIL MHATRE***

"DAD GIVE UP HIS ALL DESIRE TO FULFIL YOUR DESIRE"

He is soft hearted guy, he is different kind of person by heart and mind too. He is simple guy and try to understand your feelings. The only person in your life who never hurt you and never dream about that.

He always lost in his world and his world is you. If there anything is important for him is that you. He every time get emotional when he think about you he worry about your future and he knows that nobody care about you after him. He dedicate every moments of his life to you that's dad for you and his emotions

EVERY DAD HAS VISION THAT MATIVATE THEM TO WORK HARD

AND YOUR DAD IS ONE OF THEM FEEL PROUD TO HAVE DAD....

6. VISION

Vision this word create by dad. Every dad is visionary and his Vision isn't only for better lifestyle but creating magical life for you, his vision for you is beyond your imagination. Today very few dad get value & attention for their vision from kids, this is fact of our life.

Dad has precious vision for you and better than you. He dedicate himself such way to create beautiful & valuable vision. He stared making vision from before your birth. He very passionately does everything for you, he never get tried while doing anything his vision to be fully active for you and always be with you.

- ***DAD THE REAL HERO / BY NIKHIL MHATRE***

He has many small vision that's fulfilling your life with happiness. He make many compromise for you, but this is also part of his vision that he has for you, his vision is special like him.

He wants to see you happy and if you remember sometimes he does stupid activity just for bring smile on your face, sometimes he give you surprises, and sometimes he take you for long drive or take you at your favourite place. He try many things to make you happy. He wants to give you feeling that how special you for him and his fights for you many times, many ways to protect you keep safe but you're totally unaware about that.

- ***DAD THE REAL HERO / BY NIKHIL MHATRE***

He work hard every day he putting extra effort to earn some extra money with intention to give good & quality education, he compromise to take you up and he love you unconditionally to make you feel special. You re arrival in his life is very beautiful thing happened ever.

You're not just special for him. You're his life line. He wants see you doing great activity in your life. Helping needy people to improve their lives. Getting blessing from people. He is taking breathe only for that moments. In his entire life he dedicate everything to you also even his breathe. That show how beautiful vision he has for you.

- ***DAD THE REAL HERO / BY NIKHIL MHATRE***

Today very rare to see any dad getting respect from his kids. But many reason are responsible for that we are going into new world. Now everything is changing. Today Every second brings new changes in our life.

Change is good but the way today changing everything. That's not good for us and our next generation. Change is part of our life. Yeah it's true everyone must accept that but the way everything is changing that's not acceptable,

Now this is burning question we have, how could we forgetting sacrifice of dads, dedication, love that he give for us. He made many compromise for us. Today very few family living together because of modern thoughts, lifestyle And fights for position that's very horrible. We living our life stressfully, now nobody is happy we have invent many new things but we getting more dependable on technology whenever our parents wants to spend time with us. Especially dad today we are not giving him sufficient time because dad need your time.

"The most expensive thing is time"

Dad the visionary man who work hard for you, but get zero value for his hard work from you that he does for you. he keep smile on face no matter how hurt he is but you always find that beautiful smile on his face that's very difficult to maintain your mind every time but he does it well. He always keep himself well and try to project himself into positive way. Exactly he want you do better things in your life

Dad the way he dream about its all different and extra ordinary. Dad vision also extra ordinary.

Dad this ward is extra ordinary then actually person must be extra ordinary. There many extra ordinary vision your dad having in his mind but he need your attention just to do something special but

- *DAD THE REAL HERO / BY NIKHIL MHATRE*

DAD NEVER DOES ANYTHING SPECIAL

BUT

WHATEVER HE DOES FOR YOU BECOME SPECIAL

Dad is something like this he never say anything but he does everything for a reason.

You don't have idea when he became your helping hand, when he solve your problem. His vision to see you successful before he die. He has many tiny vision that fulfilling your life with happiness. The only thing is in his mind to give all those things and memories to you that he never had in his childhood.

Dad always praying to god to keep you safe. After your mom there is dad is the only one who is pray for you.

He isn't only pray but he protect you from every problem. His vison is to be dream dad for you.

There are many difficult task he does for you being your dad this is one of the biggest task he does and this task never going to end because dad this role is endless.

- ***DAD THE REAL HERO / BY NIKHIL MHATRE***

There is nobody would take care for you but every time he care for you. Taking care is easy but proving that's true and keeping that care forever is difficult but for dad its part of his vision.

He also creating your each and every moments memorable. Whenever you want something he try to get that thing for you. Dad the only person in your life.

Dad's love, dedication, sacrifice, emotions and vision creating your dream life. So from today you should call him

DAD THE REAL HERO

- ***DAD THE REAL HERO / BY NIKHIL MHATRE***

www.ingramcontent.com/pod-product-compliance
Lightning Source LLC
LaVergne TN
LVHW070942160826
845679LV00022B/1884
* 9 7 9 8 8 9 7 2 4 4 8 7 4 *